M000084348

MOMS KICK BUTT

MOMS KICK BUTT

31 REFLECTIONS FROM MATTHEW

Dianne Bright

CrossLink Publishing

CrossLink Publishing
1601 Mt. Rushmore Rd, STE 3288
Rapid City, SD 57702

Ordering Information:
Quantity sales. Special discounts are available on quantity purchases
by corporations, associations, and others. For details, contact the
"Special Sales Department" at the address above.

Moms Kick Butt/Bright —1st ed.

ISBN 978-1-63357-300-0

Library of Congress Control Number: 2019956944

First edition: 10 9 8 7 6 5 4 3 2 1

Published in association with Cyle Young of C.Y.L.E. (Cyle Young Literary Elite, LLC), a literary agency.

Praise for *Moms Kick Butt*

Moms Kick Butt is a devotional for moms who love Jesus and want a book that keeps it real. Insightful, funny and full of wisdom into God's word, *Moms Kick Butt* takes the reader through the book of Matthew with real life applications written with the challenges and blessings of motherhood in mind.

—**Nicole Robinson**, mom and women's Bible study teacher at The Grove Community Church in southern California

Moms Kick Butt gets to the heart of where we live as women. Our busy days tend to call us away from God and His desire for our time and attention. In these short but powerful daily applications from the book of Matthew, Dianne calls us back to the source of our strength and pushes us to keep our focus on Him without judging us for what pulls us away. She gently helps us refocus our hearts and minds on Him.

—**Vicki Greer**, Ed.S., mom, grandma, and teacher of children and women at Blue Ridge Christian Center in Arizona

Moms & Grandmas, if you're looking to apply God's Word to everyday experiences, this devotional is for you! Lighthearted and conversational, Dianne shares some of her story and challenges us to take the next step in faith with God.

—**Ingrid Cagwin**, Soul Care Provider for Global Workers in Germany

In *Moms Kick Butt*, Dianne does an excellent job of combining truth, humor, and thought-provoking questions to help lead to practical application for today's busy mom. Having three children of her own, she can relate to the challenges of motherhood and shares insights from her personal experiences. Since she was young, the author has walked faithfully with God through difficulties and trials and offers wisdom she has learned in this very enlightening devotional.

—**Valerie Hoover**, Navigators Church Ministries in Atlanta, Georgia

This is the next best thing to having a cup of tea with my friend, Dianne, in her homey kitchen. Brief, witty visits take you through the book of Matthew, stopping just long enough each time to point outward, inward and then upward. Whether you're reading it alongside your Bible or propped up next to your phone following a recipe, you'll be blessed. Add your own thoughts as you go along and then come back again and again. You'll have a treasure.

—**Nancy Tichy**, KidZ at Heart, Intl. in southern California

*This book is dedicated to
my mom, Kathy Tapscott*

Contents

Foreword

*B*utt was a bad word in our house growing up. Ironic, then, that I grew up to have a military husband and three boys who think any word for "bottom" is gut-splitting hilarious.

Butt is no longer a bad word.

In fact, as a mom I often feel like a tough guy: kicking butt and taking names. The names of my children, that is.

Their full names.

What a beautiful sound to a mama's ears when she yells for her child, telling everyone within earshot the child's birth certificate moniker.

But I don't feel tough on most days. Too often I feel guilty or frustrated. I feel like I'm not doing enough.

That's why these 31 reflections from Matthew are so important. It is God who refreshes our spirit. It is in Him whom we trust and find our strength.

So the next time we fail, feel depressed or exhausted, or are ready to let loose with a "Christopher-James-Johnson-Reginald-Jeremiah-Jett," we can remember that God gave these beautiful blessings to us.

And we kick butt.

--Bethany Jett, mom of boys and author of *They Call Me Mom*

Thanks to Readers

After writing for a variety of magazines and blogs, including Scholastic and Reader's Digest, I decided to apply a similar writing style to the book of Matthew, for moms and grandmas.

While I'm not an expert on faith, I feel most readers will connect with what I've written because of my honesty and vulnerability with these topics about life. While I pose questions to my readers—mostly challenges about how they are wrestling with God's word—I'm asking myself the same things first.

Moms and grandmas do so much for the world, rarely getting a bonus or award at the end of the year. They clean up spills and clip coupons, only to pay the bills that seem to have gone up from last month. But they sit with their cup of coffee or glass of merlot, wearing a smile that says it's all worth it.

In this brief section on thanks, I'd like to acknowledge you: my amazing readers (moms and grandmas—a.k.a. teachers, nurses, taxicab drivers, chefs, personal shoppers, accountants, counselors, and so much more). Well done for all you do on any given day without getting the praise you deserve. I'm here to remind you that the Lord sees you and cares. I see you too, so keep being awesome. And please, don't ever give up, regardless of how hard some days feel.

Lastly, thanks to my mom, mother-in-law, and grandmas who have taught me to turn to the Lord throughout my life. And to my sisters, cousins, and aunts who have been so encouraging along the way.

Day 1: Jerks

Even supermoms have a hard time being nice to jerks.

Verses of the Day
Matthew 5:43-44: "You have heard that it was said, 'Love your neighbor and hate your enemy.' But I tell you: Love your enemies and pray for those who persecute you..."

Application
Regardless of our supermom efforts, facing jerks throughout the day is hard. It could be the guy in the lowrider car who thinks you're not driving fast enough in your bumper-stickered mini-van, so he swerves to the middle of the two-lane road, kicking up a plethora of small rocks into your windshield. I mean, playing chicken behind the wheel just because you aren't driving like a psycho (#mentioningthisforafriend)? Who does that?

The thought might cross your mind to race him down and tell him off, but then these two verses come to mind. You take a few deep breaths and remember Jesus's words: "Love your enemies and pray for those who persecute you." Just turning to the Lord in the midst of the chaos counts for something, doesn't it? So I prayed for the guy—that he would get caught by a cop at the next stop sign—instead of chasing him down.

For real though, it can be tough to love people who mistreat us, especially when the offense is exponentially more intimate. Have you had a boss who threw you under the bus when she could have promoted you instead? What about a friend from Bible study who gossips behind your back? Or the relative who stays offended over a misunderstanding from months ago? In each challenging situation, let's keep it simple. Begin by 1) rejecting a hateful attitude in the midst of the difficulty, and 2) praying something kind for that person (not for them to get scooped up by a tornado or consumed by flames).

It may not bring world peace overnight, but how can you do something small today? Can you pray for someone who has mistreated you?

My Response:

Day 2: Prayer

Moms sometimes think prayer is confusing.

Verses of the Day:
Matthew 6:9-13: "This, then, is how you should pray: 'Our Father in heaven, hallowed be your name, your kingdom come, your will be done, on earth as it is in heaven. Give us today our daily bread. Forgive us our debts, as we also have forgiven our debtors. And lead us not into temptation, but deliver us from the evil one.'"

Application:
As good Christian moms, we know we are supposed to pray. But at times, we wonder if we are asking for too much or too little. Does God even want me to have the thing I'm asking for? Are some things too silly to pray about?

Drumroll, please! Jesus gives us such great tips. When we break the Lord's prayer down to its key words, we are left with eleven nouns: Father, name, kingdom, will, earth, heaven, bread, debts, debtors, temptation, and the evil one.

In the first half of the prayer, after "Our Father," the possessive adjective *your* stands out, as in "your name," "your kingdom," and "your will." That means the focus is totally on God, not us.

In the second half, the possessive adjective reverts to *our*, as in "our bread," "our debts," and "our debtors." The shift in language is significant because God wants to hear about our needs. But do you think acknowledging the order matters?

Can you focus on him first—honoring his name, thinking about what his will might be, and grasping heavenly concerns? Then, make your personal needs known, like having enough food, asking forgiveness for your wrongdoings, and seeking deliverance when you're being tempted.

How can you focus on prayer this week? Can you start by focusing on God first before your own needs?

My Response:

Day 3: Sales

Moms love sales.

Verses of the Day:
Matthew 6:19-21: "Do not store up for yourselves treasures on earth, where moth and rust destroy, and where thieves break in and steal. But store up for yourselves treasures in heaven, where thieves do not break in and steal. For where your treasure is, there your heart will be also."

Application:
This one is going to be a lot harder for some of you than for others. To be honest, I'm not a huge shopaholic, but my gosh—when something is on sale, I'm like a kid in a candy store. The point is: stuff! Do we need it, and can we take it with us when we die? NOPE! This verse makes that crystal clear.

But it sounds kind of dramatic, right? I mean, is it actually saying that shopping is a sin? Or that loving a good sale is wrong? Of course not! I think this passage is mostly a heart issue.

We know we can't take the clothes and shoes from our closets with us to heaven. Or our cars or jewelry! Not even all those first edition autographed books filling the shelves downstairs. But is the head knowledge enough? Maybe it's more than that.

Something about pursuing the real treasure, perhaps? The kind that thieves can't break in and steal? For each of us, that pursuit looks a little different. For a friend, it could be giving money to an orphanage in Africa instead of buying diamond earrings. For someone else, it might mean skipping plastic surgery and using the money for a homeless ministry at church instead. For me, it's about making sure my internal value comes from God and not what others say about me. Accolades can be robbed, but his view of me never changes. What does this look like for you? How is God shifting your attitude about the real treasure?

My Response:

Day 4: Worr

Moms worry a lot.

Verse of the Day:
Matthew 6:34: "Therefore do not worry about tomorrow, for to-morrow will worry about itself. Each day has enough trouble of its own."

Application:
There's a hilarious post going around on social media lately. It's a series of pictures of what a mom assumes when her son or daughter hasn't texted back. Is she trapped in an elevator? Has he been abducted by the mob? Have the kids sunk in quicksand or been eaten by an alligator? I made a few of these up but it's too fun, because it's totally me! I'm a professional worrier.

That makes this verse hard! The general point is similar to the adage, "One day at a time." It's also kind of like the saying that (in the nice version), "Stuff happens!" But it's more than both of these, isn't it? The key isn't just avoiding stressful thoughts, it's about jumping above to verse thirty-three, which says, "But seek first his kingdom and his righteousness, and all these things will be given to you as well."

The point is *attitude.* I'm sure a bunch of motivational posters just popped into your head, like the confident mountain climber flexing in the background or the sleek dolphins effortlessly rid-ing the waves.

Seriously though, what if we were to put God's kingdom first even in our stressful moments? In the scary moments, waiting for that late-night phone call? Sitting in the doctor's office to get the results? Going another month without a job offer?

y focusing our hearts and minds on God's promises, we will
tually feel less worried. Have you filled up a cup of water and
noticed there's only room for so much liquid? It's the same with
worrying. For today, can you put your attention on what's above?
What are a few examples of "and all these things will be given to
you" in your own life? Do you want peace? How about joy?

My Response:

Day 5: Judging Others

Moms can get pretty "judgy" of other people.

Verses of the Day:
Matthew 7:1-2: "Do not judge, or you too will be judged. For in the same way you judge others, you will be judged, and with the measure you use, it will be measured to you."

Application:
This one literally gets tough, because in what follows, Jesus talks about looking at a speck of sawdust in your sibling's eye but not paying attention to the plank in your own eye. Now, when I think of going to Home Depot or Lowe's, I can picture the wood section, and it's kind of overwhelming. The pieces are too big to carry away, so you either need to have them cut there in the store or load them onto a special cart that can handle the awkward load. To do either of those things, I would want some heavy-duty leather utility gloves to avoid the splinters.

In the case of judging others, I think we have to do the same thing. We need to grab some spiritual gloves and put them on. In this case, it's the LOVE of Christ. I don't think this passage is saying we should justify sinful behaviors, but rather that we should be very careful about making a judgment on someone else in the first place.

In other words, we should pause and pray over it—sometimes even for days or weeks. Why? Because we need time for God's love to remind us of how much he loves this same person we are judging. Then, in the right timing and with guidance from his Spirit, we can enter into the situation with new wisdom.

Naturally, we've all blown it at times. We think we are helping the person by reminding them of how horrible they are. Or we think we are saving them from hell—that one gets pretty popular. But let's make sure our Sovereign Judge sees how much we love his son or daughter first. Even if our judgment turns out to be accurate, let's focus on how their sin is actually breaking God's heart. Do you remember how much he loves them? How can you show kindness this week to a friend who has made some bad choices?

My Response:

Day 6: Talkers

Most moms talk a lot.

Verse of the Day:
Matthew 7:7: "Ask and it will be given to you; seek and you will find; knock and the door will be opened to you."

Application:
Isn't this amazing? We can ask for anything, and then it will show up at our front door like getting something from Amazon Prime? Okay, maybe it doesn't work exactly like that. But the passage does say, "Ask and it will be given to you," and the seeking and knocking stuff sound pretty good too. So, what's our takeaway?

The point seems to be focused on how our communication with him changes us, but it's not obvious at first glance. Why would God want us to ask, seek, and knock? From a practical standpoint, he wants to hear from us. Plus, it's a comforting reminder that he will always be there for us, to chat over a cup of coffee—or tea if that's your preference—and even to catch our tears. But while the Lord loves to hear us talk, it doesn't necessarily mean he's going to give us the answer(s) we are looking for.

Where have you struggled with this? Have you asked for something, then waited for months or maybe even decades? For some, it's an adult son or daughter who remains addicted to drugs. For another, it's trudging through singlehood when she really wants to be a wife and mom. Maybe something derailed your career early on? Or a friend divorced the man of her dreams?

While it's important to trust in God's promises, this passage gets tricky because we have to remember it's mostly about him, not us. And though this verse does address "you" three times, jumping ahead to verse twelve, we read, "So in everything, do to others what you would have them do to you, for this sums up the Law and the Prophets." Notice how the focus switches from *you* to *others*. That means at least part of this passage is saying the focus isn't just on our own needs. Which relative or friend can you pray for today?

My Response:

Day 7: Forgiven

*Sometimes, moms forget how much they've
been forgiven.*

Verse of the Day:
Matthew 7:13: "Enter through the narrow gate. For wide is the gate and broad is the road that leads to destruction, and many enter through it."

Application:
This reminds me of a few dystopian novels where zombies chase the protagonists, but I'm pretty sure that's not what Jesus means here. Anyway, if the image is helpful, run with it.

The following verse talks about the small gate and the narrow road leading to life, concluding with, "only a few find it." In general, I take this passage to be about salvation. But we can also view it more generally by seeing the people who are traveling down the broad road that leads to destruction as actual people whom God loves.

While some may use this verse as a weapon, it's important to consider the most effective means of sharing the love of Christ so that these lost people will actually want to "enter through the narrow gate." Consider whether we make outsiders feel so far gone that they can't possibly think of crossing over into our lane.

The good news is that there is in fact a narrow gate that we can lead people toward. When God sees the wide gate, his heart is saddened by how many people choose it. And I'd hate to miss his heart on this. That means we need to share the gospel of Christ in the most effective way possible.

How have you struggled with sharing the gospel message with others? Does God's love remind you of what you've been forgiven from? What are some ways you can help others to see the goodness of the narrow option? Who can you invite to Bible study this week? If you're not meeting with a group of gals, can you go onto the church website to get more connected today?

My Response:

Day 8: Being Real

Moms have a hard time being vulnerable.

Verses of the Day:
Matthew 8:1-3: "When he came down from the mountainside, large crowds followed him. A man with leprosy came and knelt before him and said, 'Lord, if you are willing, you can make me clean.' Jesus reached out his hand and touched the man. 'I am willing,' he said. 'Be clean!' Immediately he was cured of his leprosy."

Application:
Can you picture how intimate the setting is here? The man would likely have been used to hiding from society, probably avoiding the light of day as much as possible. But when Jesus came to town, the man endured the shame of public opinion. He knew what could happen if Jesus noticed him—that he might be cured. So, he risked it all.

I often wonder why God chooses to heal one person but not another. Is it their simple faith that brings on the miracle? Clearly, we don't think Jesus loves one of his children more than another, but something special set this man apart. Maybe it was the way he knelt before Jesus and the humility that said, "if you are willing." The man wasn't angry in his tone, nor did he blame God for the disease. Rather, he was confident because he knew the Lord could make him clean.

I know as moms we can sometimes put self-centered demands on God. We even begin to doubt his goodness or other promises from Scripture simply because things aren't turning out the way we want them to. How have you struggled with asking for healing for yourself or a loved one? Maybe there has been a time when someone you know has received healing from the Lord.

Perhaps you need healing for something less obvious. Is it depression or anxiety? Is resentment or bitterness weighing you down? Ask God to make you clean, if he is willing. Just try to be real about where you're at.

My Response:

Day 9: Bad Mommy

Jesus loves even the most horrible moms.

Verse of the Day:
Matthew 8:30: "Some distance from them a large herd of pigs was feeding. The demons begged Jesus, 'If you drive us out, send us into the herd of pigs.'"

Application:
This particular passage about Jesus healing the two demon-possessed men coming from the tombs might seem insignificant, but it stands out to me as a reminder that Jesus was even thoughtful toward demons begging for mercy. They knew who he was right away and recognized their fate because of it. But they asked for a favor anyway, and Jesus had mercy on them.

Granted, the herd rushed down the bank into the lake and drowned, but that's not the point I'm trying to make here. When have you felt like you could no longer turn to the Lord? Like you had just blown it too big-time to seek some of his mercy? Well, this story is a great reminder of how much he cares.

We see how he cared for the two possessed men being tormented by the demons. And we also see how he took the time to listen to the demons. In both instances, Jesus reveals how in tune he is with the world around us. It might seem like he's up on his throne in heaven just twiddling his thumbs, but this is a reminder of how actively he observes and listens to what's going on.

As moms, sometimes we massively fail. We lose our temper or say harsh words. It can feel like all the good we do is undone by one horrible afternoon. And yet, the Lord whispers, "Let me free you from the demon of guilt." He just wants us to come back into his presence.

Do you feel like maybe he just doesn't care? Are you hiding from God because you've done too many bad things to receive his mercy? Even the demons reached out, so it's never too late to turn back to the Lord. Jesus forgives bad moms too.

My Response:

Day 10: Dialing 911

Even moms need to call the doctor from time to time.

Verses of the Day:
Matthew 9:12-13: "On hearing this, Jesus said, 'It is not the healthy who need a doctor, but the sick. But go and learn what this means: I desire mercy, not sacrifice. For I have not come to call the righteous, but sinners.'"

Application:
Did Jesus really come to hang out with sinners? That just feels unfair, doesn't it? It's as if there's a cool kids' club—where the bad boys wear leather and the girls hike their skirts up too high—at their secret hangout. I may have placed this back at the Grease musical, but you get the point.

Wouldn't Jesus rather sit at the prim and proper table with those good girls and boys who cross their Ts and dot their Is? Doesn't he see the mom who always volunteers as room-mom and the one who heads up the PTA? What about those people?

First off, this passage addresses sick people—and it's important to remember that we are all sick. That means we all need a savior, even the ones who look squeaky clean on the outside.

Then there's this part about Jesus desiring mercy and not sacrifice. Where do we go with that? The word that pops into my head is *understanding*. I think Jesus is saying, "Try to understand sick people, rather than just seeing them as sick." While we may not feel sick today, spiritually speaking, it wasn't that long ago when we too were lost and in need of a savior.

The last section of this passage talks about Jesus coming to call sinners, not people who are already righteous. Now, I don't think that means he doesn't have time for those who already follow him. But it reflects his heart, which yearns for all to find salvation. He goes back for the one lost sheep, remember?

Do you think you're better than someone else? Perhaps you need help? How is God shifting your attitude? Who can you be praying for this week?

My Response:

Day 11: Miracles

Moms pray for crazy stuff every day.

Verses of the Day:
Matthew 11:4-5: "Jesus replied, 'Go back and report to John what you hear and see: The blind receive sight, the lame walk, those who have leprosy are cured, the deaf hear, the dead are raised, and the good news is preached to the poor.'"

Application:
It's one of those *wow* passages, right? I mean, who in modern day times has seen sight returned to a blind person? Or a paralyzed person just up and walking again? We don't deal with leprosy on this side of the globe as much as some, but what about someone being cured from stage 4 cancer? Then it just gets crazy. Dead people are coming to life? How could that be? It's too amazing even for my friends who love zombie shows, because it just doesn't happen in real life...or does it?

Some of you are nodding, like physically moving your head up and down, because you know this stuff is real. You've prayed it. You've seen it firsthand. But others are dubious because it's too unbelievable to even pray for in the first place.

Miracles do in fact occur throughout the world on a regular basis. They don't usually make the news headlines, but they fill the social media reels pretty well. And while some of them might be made up, many of them are actually very real. In my own life, I've experienced some actual, concrete miracles that would be hard to explain to a nonbeliever—speaking in tongues, a vision from the Lord after my stepdad died, and seeing a child healed from a serious medical condition.

Our response is twofold. First, we must be open to the idea of God performing miracles. Jesus performed them here on earth more than two thousand years ago, and he can still do them today. Second, we must be patient enough to wait on God's will and timing. How can you practice praying bigger and waiting on God?

My Response:

Day 12: Zonked

Moms are so wiped out.

Verses of the Day:
Matthew 11:28-30: "Come to me, all you who are weary and burdened, and I will give you rest. Take my yoke upon you and learn from me, for I am gentle and humble in heart, and you will find rest for your souls. For my yoke is easy and my burden is light."

Application:
There is a lot going on here, so let's break this down. Preceding this passage, Jesus denounces the cities where all the miracles had just been performed, because they wouldn't repent. Then he jumps to the fact that children grasp these kinds of things way better than supposedly wise and learned adults. He goes on to say that no one knows him except the Father, and vice versa. Then, like he's slowing down a whirlwind of chaos, he says, "Come to me, all you who are weary and burdened..."

The gist of today's passage is that moms can definitely turn to Jesus when they are tired and overwhelmed. The result will be rest. And while it's especially awesome to know that Jesus can handle our physical tiredness, remember that he can also handle our mental exhaustion. Most moms can relate to the act of collapsing into bed, but what about your mind? All that whining from the day adds up, right? The demands are just too much, and you start grabbing for that glass of merlot, because it's five o'clock somewhere. But what if Jesus can offer more than that full-bodied glass of grapes ever could?

He can! Let's go back to the text. He sees us and our struggles, then reminds us, "I am gentle and humble in heart..." This is the part where you take a deep breath and go, "He sees me for who I am, right where I'm at." Then, it gets even better. Jesus says, "...and you will find rest for your souls." So, it's even more than him understanding our physical and emotional needs. When our souls feel worn out, he gets us on an even deeper level.

How are you coping? Can you give some of your burdens over to the Lord today? Just say, "Help me!"

My Response:

Day 13: Gardening

All moms are shallow—sometimes.

Verses of the Day:
Matthew 13:4-6: "As [the farmer] was scattering the seed, some fell along the path, and the birds came and ate it up. Some fell on rocky places, where it did not have much soil. It sprang up quickly, because the soil was shallow. But when the sun came up, the plants were scorched, and they withered because they had no root."

Application:
Most of us read this passage waiting for the next two verses. In fact, it feels funny skipping the part about the super bad seed that falls among thorns, which grows up and chokes the plant. Then—ahhh—drumroll, please: we get to the climax about the good seed falling on good soil, where it produces an amazing crop—even more than the farmer could have imagined.

Don't we all want to be the good seed? But how often are we the shallow seed or the seed that falls in with the thorns? Let's just be honest. Sometimes we look so good on the outside, others might see us and think we're always the good seed with the flowery Instagram feed. The smiles. The Bible verses. The new shoes. The yummy salmon dish we just cooked to perfection.

But what's underneath that highlight reel? Are you hiding some stuff about your marriage from those closest to you? What about grabbing food or a pill when no one sees because it comforts you? How about that second glass of wine, when one would have sufficed?

The thing is, Jesus knows who we really are. He sees us deep down, and on any given day, we could be any of the three types of seed. We could be shallow, super bad, or amazing! And he loves us regardless, but the only way we can grow with other believers is by being honest about the state of our actual garden.

Can you share some of your struggles with a friend who will pray for you?

My Response:

Day 14: Boundaries

*Sometimes moms struggle the most with their
own families.*

Verses of the Day:
Matthew 13:57-58: "And they took offense at him. But Jesus said
to them, 'Only in his hometown and in his own house is a prophet
without honor.' And he did not do many miracles there because
of their lack of faith."

Application:
This passage follows an account of people questioning Jesus's
abilities, asking stuff like, "How's this guy so cool and powerful?" They basically say, "Isn't he just a nobody? How did he get
so lucky?" The people got offended, and Jesus got sad, knowing
people from his own town wouldn't give him the benefit of the
doubt.

How often do we as moms feel convicted about something
in our guts but feel like we have to defend it to the people who
know us best? It could be any one of a gazillion things, ranging
from child-rearing to which stain remover works best to vaccina-
tions. But whatever the case, it's hard to feel misunderstood by
those closest to us.

It's basically impossible to avoid offending some people, but
we can control how we respond. Jesus didn't sweep his emotions
under the rug and act like the people taking offense didn't bug
him. Instead, he held back some of his favor from them, indi-
cated by the fact that he did not do many miracles there because
of their lack of faith.

Whether you're in a toxic situation or just one that makes you uncomfortable, it's okay to put up a healthy boundary. If you constantly feel criticized or put down, you can say to the other person, "I don't like being talked to in that way." In the middle of a disagreement, it's okay to say, "I need to get some air," before stepping outside to pray for a bit.

Do you offend anyone by the way you do things? How can you set up better emotional boundaries for yourself, even in your own family?

My Response:

Day 15: Penny-Pinchers

Moms can squeeze every penny out of each dollar.

Verses of the Day:
Matthew 14:19-20: "Taking the five loaves and the two fish and looking up to heaven, he gave thanks and broke the loaves. Then he gave them to the disciples, and the disciples gave them to the people. They all ate and were satisfied, and the disciples picked up twelve basketfuls of broken pieces that were left over."

Application:
This scene is hard to imagine. Maybe it would be easier if instead of five loaves and two fish, it said five footlong subs from Subway and two Caesar salad bags from Costco. Either way, the result is amazing. By doing what Jesus asked them to do, the disciples ended up with more than they started with.

It's natural to worry that if we give a monetary gift or take someone a meal, somehow, we might come up short by the end of the month. But this story demonstrates that when you follow God's prompting to help someone else, you always come out ahead. In other words, God makes the math add up.

As moms, we literally stretch each dollar, squeezing out every possible penny. Your cell is overflowing with digital wallet coupons, and BOGOs are celebrated like holidays. Free shipping with Prime goes without saying. But we can get consumed by the deals and the bills and the to-do lists that are still with us by the end of the month. It might even scare us into avoiding the Holy Spirit's promptings to help out those in need.

If we ignore God's whisper, it could mean missing out on God's blessings. He had the ability to feed five thousand men, plus the women and children who weren't even counted, with just five loaves and two fish.

How can you stretch yourself to trust that God will come through for your needs this week? Is he prompting you to help a family in need this month? Just look up to heaven and give thanks. Then, do the right thing.

My Response:

Day 16: Mom Language

Sometimes moms cuss.

Verses of the Day:
Matthew 15:18-19: "But the things that come out of the mouth come from the heart, and these make a man (or woman) 'unclean.' For out of the heart come evil thoughts, murder, adultery, sexual immorality, theft, false testimony, slander."

Application:
Raise your hand if something worse than *hell* or *damn* comes out of your mouth on occasion! I know I'm not the only one. And as much as I try to use euphemisms instead of the really bad words, it does happen from time to time. My kids will be the first to tell you their favorite joke is, "Don't use mom language." For the record, I'm actually getting better.

So, let's dive into this with honest hearts. Do the words matter that much? I think the right answer is obvious: Yes, they matter. But what's even more important is having a healthy heart. If you're the mom just thinking the cuss words in your head but not saying them, this might apply to you even more. The meat of this passage is what comes after the mouth stuff: evil thoughts, murder, adultery, sexual immorality, theft, false testimony, and slander.

Most of us don't see ourselves struggling with the bad stuff like murder, adultery, sexual immorality, or theft. But what about bad thoughts, like picturing the car that just cut you off on the freeway careening off into a ditch? Or what about the ten dollars the clerk overpaid you—not that big of a deal, but still, not quite right! Then, there's the bit about slander, or making a false or damaging statement about someone. How about making yourself look better than someone else because you feel jealous of her? Or throwing her under the bus after Bible study, then feeling sort of bad about it later?

Don't ignore the bigger sins though—they can creep up on you too. All are issues of the heart. Can you turn to Jesus today and be authentic with him?

My Response:

Day 17: Head Space

Moms are dramatic.

Verses of the Day:
Matthew 16:25-26: "For whoever wants to save (her) life will lose it, but whoever loses (her) life for me will find it. What good will it be for a (wo)man if (s)he gains the whole world, yet forfeits (her) soul? Or what can a (wo)man give in exchange for (her) soul?"

Application:
Talk about dramatic! First, saving your life really means having to lose it first? And gaining the world actually takes forfeiting your soul? The last part makes the most sense; we know we have nothing to offer in exchange for our soul. Just Jesus! And that's the main point!

Every time, it comes back to him. Only he can save your life. The more you press into his presence, the more obvious this becomes. Lose the must-do lists of what makes this life meaningful. Let him write the agenda instead, even if it means cutting out one last meeting of the day or one less acquisition for the month.

One way of looking at this is to picture your tombstone. What do you want it to say? *Workaholic and stress-case, mom of three, blah blah blah, oh—and she loved Jesus.* Let the part about your commitment to God come first. The rest will fall into place.

Trust me, I get it. Bills have to be paid. Food has to be prepared and put on the table. Floors have to be mopped, and rugs vacuumed. But let the obsessions fall to the wayside. Put God in the first part of your day and let it end with his love as well. Create enough head space so you can hear from his Spirit throughout the day. That's what having a healthy soul is really about.

How can you live today for eternity? Is there a way to do ten percent less on your to-do or be-amazing lists? What about making a little bit more time for prayer and diving into God's word this week—even a five-minute devo with the hubs?

My Response:

Day 18: Freaked Out

Moms are afraid of the boogie man—and
everything else, too.

Verses of the Day:
Matthew 17:6-7: "When the disciples heard this, they fell face-down to the ground, terrified. But Jesus came and touched them. 'Get up,' he said. 'Don't be afraid.'"

Application:
My list of fears is too long to write out. Though I ask God to protect my family multiple times per day, it's hard not to fear the world and every bad thing and person in it. From the headlines we hear when the alarm clock goes off to the social media feeds scrolling all day long, it's like a dark cloud of bad news is looming overhead. Why? A lot of it's true, and that's the sad part—bad stuff really does happen to good people.

But, in spite of all the crap, we still have a safe place to turn—to Jesus. Now, you may have been wondering about this part of today's passage. What do the disciples hear that makes them fall facedown to the ground, terrified? Preceding this passage, we read about the transfiguration, where the Father's voice and being enveloped by a bright cloud freak the disciples out. Our heavenly Father explains that Jesus is his Son, whom he loves and with whom he is pleased.

Maybe being in the Father's presence makes them afraid of being seen for what they aren't? He's holy; they are not. But, interestingly, after they fall down, Jesus touches them, which must have offered some amount of comfort. He then tells them not to be afraid. After that, they look up and see only Jesus there with them.

The message of this passage is twofold. First, Jesus totally understands us when we are feeling afraid. Second, he gets personal, touching the deepest part of our pain (often the thing that is actually causing us to be afraid of a new situation or person). After meeting us where we're at, he tells us, "I'm bigger than this. Trust me, even though it's scary."

How can you let Jesus meet you in the scary places of life? Will you let him touch that painful part of your heart? Can you share this fear with another mom?

My Response:

Day 19: Stay Young

Moms can be kids at heart.

Verses of the Day:
Matthew 18:3-4: "And he said, 'I tell you the truth, unless you change and become like little children, you will never enter the kingdom of heaven. Therefore, whoever humbles (herself) like this child is the greatest in the kingdom of heaven.'"

Application:
Kids dive into finger paints like professional Monets, unworried about what people will think. They eat sugar like it's a primary food group, whining when a parent steps in with veggies or a protein shake instead. Children curl into your hug like their skin could melt into your own. Even their not-so-cute tantrums and wrestling matches are done wholeheartedly. I think that's why Jesus focuses on coming to heaven like a little child—with simple faith and fully committed!

It sounds great, but how often do we come to him like that? Fully charged, enraptured by his every word, hanging onto his arms, jumping up and down to get closer to his face so he can hear us better? Crying because our juice box spilled and someone stole our crayon?

Let's face it, that's who we are sometimes—sad because a friend didn't invite us to that movie date or the gal's night out that everyone plastered onto Instagram. Mad because a younger coworker got promoted above us, because she had more technological experience. What then? Do we race to Jesus like a child? Do we go to him first, or to food, a pill, or a glass of merlot?

As we approach heaven's gate—though we aren't quite there yet—let's focus on two things from this passage: *change* and *humility*. We have to change and become like little kids, and we must humble ourselves. We aren't that amazing, but Jesus is—so let's look to him instead of our circumstances.

How can you be more childlike today? Can you trust God for something that feels impossible? Can you unclench your fists and reach for his hug?

My Response:

Day 20: Cliques

Moms go to the bathroom in groups.

Verses of the Day:
Matthew 18:19-20: "Again, I tell you that if two of you on earth agree about anything you ask for, it will be done for you by my Father in heaven. For where two or three come together in my name, there am I with them."

Application:
The adage "power in numbers" comes to mind, but this passage is about more than that. I'm not sure it literally means that if you pray with someone else about anything, it's going to happen either. I mean, I could pray with my table gals that Aquaman would be the guest speaker next week at Bible study, but I don't think that's going to happen. Pretty sure they'll know how to pray for me too—#lust.

I think it means God loves seeing us in community. We can't do life alone. It's way too hard and lonely. Even with a strong extended family, a wonderful spouse, and fabulous children, we need to fellowship with other believers. It's not enough to have a nice relative constantly texting you that she's praying for you. You need to meet regularly with other women from your community to pray and study God's word. If you want to host a group, that's great! It doesn't have to happen at a church, but it needs to be on your calendar.

Of course, God hears us when we pray by ourselves. But it's powerful to think he takes extra special notice of us when we are in a group. It's the whole point of the Trinity—Father, Son, and

Spirit as one. When we pray in a group, we are many different personalities, but united under the same Spirit.

If you are in a group, how can you encourage someone new to join? If you aren't in a study with other women, what is keeping you away? Do you feel like you aren't good enough? Do you think you will be asked to pray or read out loud? Just remember, God said it matters, so go for it! If your table group stinks, switch to mine. Jason Momoa's wife is totally welcome too!

My Response:

Day 21: Doers

Moms accomplish a ton every day.

Verse of the Day:
Matthew 19:26: "Jesus looked at them and said, 'With man this is impossible, but with God all things are possible.'"

Application:
If you've given birth, you already know you're basically Captain Marvel. But even if you had a surrogate or were blessed through adoption, you know that you're a bad-xxx too. I had to say it, cuz it's true. Moms do so much. It's like, "Sure, I can bake five dozen cookies and carpool ten kids in my eight-person van, in the next forty minutes, cuz someone's gotta do it. Why not me?"

You know how you can stack stuff on your body to take a load upstairs better than Gumby (remember him?) or the Flash? Three piles of clothes and towels, plus five water bottles huddled under your armpits, four books below the clothes, and a side of freshly made organic guacamole and chips in the crick of your neck for the hubs watching the game in the bonus room. And then, "Sure, I can grab more salsa."

It's as if we could modify this verse and say, "With moms, all things are possible." But herein lies the problem. We are doers, all the way. We go from green to red, then collapse into bed. But I'm pretty sure God has a different plan for us. A better plan! One that involves yellow, not just green and red.

As women of God, we are called to depend upon his strength throughout the day. That means we have to push the pause button and not feel bad about it. The passage prior to this verse is about it being easier for a camel to go through the eye of a needle than for a rich person to enter the kingdom of heaven. It's interesting that it has to do with money, especially when most moms are obsessed with money—not in an evil way, but in an I've-memorized-every-dollar-we-need-to-spend kind of way. Achievements are good too. Otherwise, who would fill the fridge and cook dinner? The part that seems to matter most is the attitude of the heart: focusing on God's strength for the money stuff and the to-do items.

So, how can you let God do more? Where can you slow down a bit?

My Response:

Day 22: The Comparison Game

Moms compare themselves and their
circumstances to other moms.

Verses of the Day:
Matthew 20:13-14: "But he answered one of them, 'Friend, I am not being unfair to you. Didn't you agree to work for a denarius? Take your pay and go. I want to give the (wo)man who was hired last night the same as I gave you.'"

Application:
This passage deals with the workers in a vineyard. Not too shabby, right? Pick some grapes, grab a glass of merlot on break, and pull out your cheese board. But that's not what's going on here. Instead, the workers who have been working since the morning complain because they are paid the same amount as the guys who were hired at the end of the day, only working for one hour.

It might feel easier to relate to this passage if you consider a scene at the elementary school or middle school. The kids come home with their class schedules, then moms start posting everything on social media about how their little darling will be in math, history, and PE with so-and-so. But your kid doesn't have a single friend in ELA. And your kid also got second lunch, but most of her friends got first lunch. Then there's a fun field trip coming up, and three cliquey moms get picked for the trip, but you don't make the cut—even though you've been room-mom three years in a row now.

It might sound silly to compare these two scenarios, but how often do we make a mountain out of a molehill by distrusting God's goodness for our own lives? If we wake up and say, "God, whatever you have for me today, I receive your will and your blessings," think of how we could let some of the drama go. That means if your kid is placed at the end of the aisle for the choir concert, it's not going to stress you out, because you already lifted her up for blessings that day. Maybe something good will come out of her standing on the side, such as realizing she's not always the center of attention. She may even make a new friend.

How can you encourage your family to see things with a more trusting attitude?

My Response:

Day 23: MLM

Moms love networking.

Verses of the Day:
Matthew 21:12-13: "Jesus entered the temple area and drove out all who were buying and selling there. He overturned the tables of the money changers and the benches of those selling doves. 'It is written,' he said to them, 'My house will be called a house of prayer, but you are making it a den of robbers.'"

Application:
The "house of prayer" part of this passage references Isaiah 56:7. In discussing salvation for others—specifically foreigners and eunuchs—who love the Lord and worship him, who keep the Sabbath and who follow his covenant, God says that "these I will bring to my holy mountain and give them joy in my house of prayer. Their burnt offerings and sacrifices will be accepted on my altar; for my house will be called a house of prayer for all nations."

By looking back, we see that God's house of prayer had been a holy place and a place of joy for hundreds of years. Those same attributes extended to the temple Jesus is referencing here in Matthew, and I believe they continue into our churches today. Though we now live under the new covenant, it's important that we don't water down God's holiness.

At times, we use church events and groups to advance our own causes. We think of whom we can connect with for the growth of our own business or even a good volunteer organization. Though neither pursuit is inherently evil, we need to check our hearts when we enter the holy mountain, metaphorically speaking—the table for small group or the rows of chairs set up for service.

While it's natural to connect with fellow believers about various interests and concerns, let's make sure we give God our full attention while we're there worshiping him. Can you schedule networking details at another time instead of during church events? Can you carve out five minutes before service even starts to meditate on him—even something simple, like repeating Jesus's name?

My Response:

Day 24: Choose Ice Cream

Moms can get hung up on stupid stuff.

Verses of the Day:
Matthew 22:17-18: "'Tell us then, what is your opinion? Is it right to pay taxes to Caesar or not?' But Jesus, knowing their evil intent, said, 'You hypocrites, why are you trying to trap me?'"

Application:
In this passage, the Pharisees set this up like a trick question—knowing there wasn't really a right way to answer it. But Jesus knew their intentions and called them out. There are times in our own lives when it's worth taking the bait, but it could just end in an argument—so let's be smart about what we take on. If you and another believer have different opinions about something that is nonessential to our belief in Christ, then let it go. Differences of opinion can cost friendships and even result in people switching to a different church. Maybe there's another way.

Sure, there can be changing seasons of friendship and the church you call home. But if a split happens because of a disagreement that doesn't have to do with salvation or a core doctrinal issue, maybe it's okay to agree to disagree and go grab some ice cream together.

The passage is clearly focusing on how the Pharisees are trying to trap Jesus. In this instance, they talk about paying taxes to Caesar. In another, they complain about healing or rescuing an animal on the Sabbath. The point is, Jesus focuses on the heart of the person instead of legalism. Let's try not to miss his challenge here.

It doesn't mean we can just depend on our feelings and water down God's Word so it no longer has meaning. The Word of God certainly stands the test of time. But when it comes to how you baptize someone or whether communion becomes the actual body and blood of Christ, we could just give some space for there to be differences of opinion. A friend might even be from a more conservative denomination, choosing to wear a head covering. It feels outside the box for many of us, but why judge her for trying to honor her conviction? Let's welcome her into our group instead. How can you see people's hearts better this week?

My Response:

Day 25: Pariah

Moms sometimes have a hard time loving that
one neighbor down the street.

Verses of the Day:
Matthew 22:36-39: "'Teacher, which is the greatest commandment in the Law?' Jesus replied: 'Love the Lord your God with
all your heart and with all your soul and with all your mind. This
is the first and greatest commandment. And the second is like it:
Love your neighbor as yourself.'"

Application:
Most people can relate to the frustration of that one family down
the street who just doesn't follow the rules. Their cans aren't
brought in on time. They don't mow their lawn until the HOA
threatens them. Their teens rob neighborhood packages to resell
for profit and slash tires for fun (#mentioningthisforafriend).
And that's where it gets tough.

You might identify the house that's selling drugs in your
neighborhood, feeling an immediate urge to pull away from even
smiling as you drive by. You also get an upgraded alarm system,
which makes perfect sense. But the point is, we should be praying for that single mom trying to make ends meet, because obvi-
ously her family is weighed down by a dark spiritual battle. And
if not for the grace of God in our own families, it could be our
kids struggling with these same issues.

But on a practical level, how can you love that household when
yours might be their next target? And how could you possibly invite them to church? The truth is, it feels wrong to think hateful
things about that family on your street while doing the first part

well (loving the Lord your God with all your heart and with all your soul and with all your mind). I mean, how can we love the Lord with all our heart, soul, and mind if we are busy cursing the people that cause the most trouble?

When we are faced with other people's struggles, we should try to show compassion, because that's what Jesus does on a regular basis. Of course, he ultimately judges their shortcomings too, but we should think of how we would want people to treat our kids if they were caught up in the wrong situation. How can you show compassion to that one house down your street? Can you try to see them as Jesus does? Would you be willing to invite them to church?

My Response:

Day 26: Finishing Well

Moms need reminders of heaven.

Verses of the Day:
Matthew 24:30-31: "At that time the sign of the Son of Man will appear in the sky, and all the nations of the earth will mourn. They will see the Son of Man coming on the clouds of the sky, with power and great glory. And he will send his angels with a loud trumpet call, and they will gather his elect from the four winds, from one end of the heavens to the other."

Application:
We get so busy with sports, homework, and volunteer stuff that it sometimes feels like the whirlwind will never end. But deep down, we know a day is coming when Jesus will return. And for believers, it's great news! It means that our salvation is secure because we put our faith in him and his finished work on the cross. It means we are fully forgiven and redeemed.

It also signifies that God writes the final chapter. For all the things we couldn't control or were victims of in this lifetime, the Lord gets the last word. I mean, who hasn't been through some unfair circumstances? Some people can relate to really big injustices, like being raped or losing a child to a drunk driver. For a friend, it could be their spouse leaving them for an upgraded model. Maybe you've been overlooked for a job or a contract because of your race, gender, or beliefs. Does it feel like God has turned a blind eye to your situation(s)?

There are some things we simply won't understand on this side of heaven. The passage from 1 Corinthians 13:12 comes to mind: "Now we see but a poor reflection as in a mirror; then we shall see face to face. Now I know in part; then I shall know fully, even as I am fully known."

When we keep our eyes on his "power and great glory" and the fact that we are "fully known," we get a better perspective. How can you finish well, even when life has been unfair? Who can you share God's hope with this week?

My Response:

Day 27: Grudges

Moms hold grudges.

Verses of the Day:
Matthew 26:14-16: "Then one of the Twelve—the one called Judas Iscariot—went to the chief priests and asked, 'What are you willing to give me if I hand him over to you?' So they counted out for him thirty silver coins. From then on Judas watched for an opportunity to hand him over."

Application:
This application may seem farfetched—how could any one of us come close to being as unfaithful as Judas? But I doubt he started out with a horrible heart. More than likely, temptation crept in slowly. Perhaps he was jealous of one of the other disciples. It may have started by him being overlooked.

Picture yourself in a Bible study setting. One of the gals is asked to help with a special event because she's super creative. Maybe your leader just forgot that you happen to have a background in graphic design. Or perhaps there were ten tickets for the women's spring event, and you missed the sign-ups due to illness, but no one remembered to add your name to the list. Now the tickets are all sold out, and there's not a spot for you.

Of course, it could be a more obvious offense like someone fabricating something about your child that others start gossiping about. Then you patiently live out the repercussions with a grudge, or you leave the group for a fresh start. We can all relate to this kind of resentment. But it's important to hand it over to the Lord, because the offended party pays the price.

Just think if Judas had been more honest about his struggles. What if he had gone to Jesus and said, "Lord, I'm feeling tempted, like I might even walk away. Can you forgive me and help me to be better?" Sometimes being honest about our true feelings makes us feel weak, but it could lead to incredible healing and strength. Share a grudge you've been holding on to with the Lord. How can you let it go? Who can you forgive?

My Response:

Day 28: Wasting Time

Moms waste time on social media and binge-watching their shows.

Verses of the Day:
Matthew 26:43-45: "When he came back, he again found them sleeping, because their eyes were heavy. So he left them and went away once more and prayed the third time, saying the same thing. Then he returned to the disciples and said to them, 'Are you still sleeping and resting? Look, the hour is near, and the Son of Man is betrayed into the hands of sinners.'"

Application:
Jesus's disciples zoning out while Jesus goes away to pray before being arrested may not sound like you or me. But how farfetched is it really? How many times have we grabbed our coffee and our phones instead of our Bibles? Sounds dramatic right? But I think I'm hitting the mark here.

How many apps are open during the day before we've even thought about saying hello to the Lord? What about bingeing on our favorite shows? While social media and TV aren't in and of themselves evil, they can become sneaky idols. The problem is threefold.

First, all the screening eats up so much time that we could have used meditating on God's word. Think of just fifteen minutes each day, reading the Psalms or diving into one of Paul's letters. But often we put it off; then we become tired and weighed down by our to-do lists. We feel bad that we weren't able to carve out time for God, but we promise we'll do better tomorrow.

Second, by spending so much time on our phones and electronic devices, we start to see our own lives in a different light, thinking we need to be better than we are. With cosmetic surgery. Or a new car. Or a new husband. Or a new job. Or a new church. Sometimes, we even forget our current blessings!

Third, we miss out on relationships. Instead of actually hanging out with each other, we start to believe digital relationships are enough. Who can you hang out with this week instead of just "liking" their posts on social media?

My Response:

Day 29: Depression

Moms sometimes feel depressed, and it's okay
not to be okay.

Verses of the Day:
Matthew 27:45-46: "From the sixth hour until the ninth hour darkness came over all the land. About the ninth hour Jesus cried out in a loud voice, '*Eloi, Eloi, lama sabachthani?*'—which means, 'My God, my God, why have you forsaken me?'"

Application:
First off, we know what Jesus has gone through on the cross—not personally, but we get a pretty good idea from the preceding text and the movies we've seen. They stripped him. They mocked him. Put a crown of thorns on his head. Struck him. Made him carry his own cross. Pierced him. Crucified him. Then, they divided up his clothes. And they watched and waited.

Have you heard that voice in your own life? What about from your own heart, saying, "God, why can't you hear me? Why do I have to wait so long for your answer on this?" It likely isn't death on a cross, but it may be overcoming an addiction in your life. Or it could be the loss of a close relative—how and why would the Lord take them from you? What about a recent disability or being on an antidepressant?

As believers, we try so hard to keep it all together, wearing our happy masks every Sunday. When someone asks how she can pray for you, it's easier to say, "Well, I have this friend who needs prayer. She's really struggling." But what about admitting your own needs? Your deepest fears and anxieties?

Maybe you're in a season of personal darkness. How could you share some of your struggles with another believer this week? Would you be willing to be honest with the Lord? Tell him you're mad or sad or glad. Don't hold back; he already knows your true feelings anyway. And he understands.

My Response:

Day 30: Lesser Than

Moms matter to Jesus.

Verses of the Day:
Matthew 28:5-7: "The angel said to the women, 'Do not be afraid, for I know that you are looking for Jesus, who was crucified. He is not here; he has risen, just as he said. Come and see the place where he lay. Then go quickly and tell the disciples: He has risen from the dead and is going ahead of you into Galilee. There you will see him. Now I have told you.'"

Application:
Jesus was an early feminist—though conservative, obvs. Even back in his time, when women weren't exactly considered equals, he was their advocate. It's interesting to note the previous verse, about how the guards were so terrified of the angel that they shook and became like dead men. But that's a side point—#girlpower. Anyway, the point is, Mary Magdalene and the other Mary were calm enough to interact with the angel, and they were entrusted with some big stuff. Why? Because Jesus knew they could handle it.

First, the women hurried away from the tomb to tell the disciples. And they were filled with joy. But here's what they did not do: wait around to discuss whether or not they should obey the angel. Nor did they call up ten friends to see if it was cool or not. But it gets even better. Next, Jesus met them and spoke to them. And their response was awesome. In verse nine, it says, "They came to him, clasped his feet and worshiped him."

It's so cool that after the resurrection, Jesus counted on women to get the message out to his crew. Maybe it's because women are so task-oriented...who knows? But it's a great reminder of how much Jesus values you and me. Sometimes, even young girls can feel slighted or less important. But they never get that message from Jesus. He says, "You are valued. You matter. You are trustworthy." Let's encourage other women to grasp their true value in Christ.

Where have you been fed a lie that your life is lesser than? Can you let it go?

My Response:

Day 31: YOLO

Moms make a big difference.

Verses of the Day:
Matthew 28:18-20: "Then Jesus came to them and said, 'All authority in heaven and on earth has been given to me. Therefore go and make disciples of all nations, baptizing them in the name of the Father and of the Son and of the Holy Spirit, and teaching them to obey everything I have commanded you. And surely I am with you always, to the very end of the age.'"

Application:
The eleven disciples are waiting for Jesus at the mountain in Galilee, where he told them to go. When he shows up, this is what they hear. But it's a lot to take in. So, let's dissect some of the action words: go, make, baptize, teach, obey, and command. They sound kind of overwhelming, right? Especially if your leader was just crucified—even though it's pretty cool that he came back from the dead and all. Still, there's a good bit of hostility going around.

Deep breath—let's not forget the last part: "I am with you always." It's important to remember we are not alone. With his Spirit as our helper, we can do the things he asks of us. We can go far away if that's what God wants. Or we can stay close by; regardless of distance, we are called to step out of our comfort zone. It could be sharing him with a colleague or friend who isn't exactly open-minded.

Maybe you have never been baptized, and now is the time. Or perhaps your kids need to get baptized. Look into it at your church, and get it on your calendar, girlfriend! What about teaching others? Maybe it's your turn to volunteer with children or young adults. Or you could step up in the women's ministry. Could you host a table or help decorate?

What's holding you back from the Great Commission? How can you team up with the Lord to bring more people into his kingdom today? What will happen if you go outside your comfort zone? Maybe you're actually being called to go on a mission trip. For now, can you just attend the meeting for more info?

My Response:

A Little Bit on Prayer

It's easy to put off prayer because we feel like we aren't going to say the right thing anyway. This seems especially true in groups, where we think, "They'll say it way better than I ever could."

But, now that you've made it through thirty-one days of reflections, I want to encourage you to keep going. Spend time praying and journaling. Remember, it looks different for each believer. If you love art, you could spend some time painting the Lord a picture that reflects what you want to share with him. Maybe a nature walk is where you feel your spirit can press into his presence best.

It might be on your knees next to your Bible, and that's great too. I just want to remind you that the main thing God wants is your whole heart. By spending time with him on a regular basis, you will begin to care about what he cares about most. And that's when your life begins to look more like his—seeing the homeless person on the corner, caring about the friend going through a divorce, spending time listening to the alcoholic instead of judging her.

I'm for sure not asking you to be perfect, just challenging you to go to God as you are today. Set your watch for five minutes. Then up it to ten and maybe twenty during the following weeks. What I've found is the more I give of myself to the Lord, the more I can't hold back—because I was made in his image and made for redemption and reconciliation. He loves all of me, and that makes my life count, regardless of whatever crap is going on during any given month. Your life matters too! So, keep being awesome, moms and grandmas! The world needs you, and the Lord has placed you in it for a reason.

Asking Jesus into Your Heart

I wouldn't want anyone to finish reading this book without knowing how simple it is to start a relationship with Jesus Christ. All you need to do is acknowledge who he is and who you aren't.

You can pray this simple prayer:

> *Lord Jesus, I need you. I've fallen short in my life and can't fix myself without your help. Because of what you did on the cross, I'm asking you to forgive me for all my past, current, and future shortcomings. I want you to lead my life, and I'm choosing to follow you from now on. Amen.*

Next steps:
God is in your life now. He will never leave you, so even if you don't feel super different, trust that he is with you.

Start reading your Bible. You can begin with the book of Matthew, since you've already read some of it from this book. It's straightforward about who Jesus is and what he wants for your life. Even five minutes per day is a great goal!

Find a church in your area where the Bible is taught, and the focus is on growing closer in your relationship with Jesus. Attend regularly and start connecting with other people who want to grow in their faith as well.

Printed in the United States
By Bookmasters